GIUSEPPE BOVINI
Director of the Institute
of Ravenna and Byzantine Antiquities,
in the University of Bologna

RAVENNA

its mosaics
and monuments

A. LONGO EDITORE - RAVENNA

PREFACE

It is advisable, for practical reasons, to visit Ravenna by the following itineraries where the monuments and places of interest are grouped as follows:

1) Piazza del Popolo - The Dante Area - The Church of San Francesco - The Town Art Collection - The Church of Sant'Agata Maggiore.

2) The Cathedral - The Neone Baptistry or Cathedral Baptistry - Archiepiscopal Museum - The Archiepiscopal Chapel.

3) Galla Placidia's Mausoleum - The Basilica of St. Vitale - The National Museum.

4) The church of the Holy Ghost (ex-Arian Cathedral) - Arian Baptistry - The Church of St. John the Evangelist - St. Apollinare Nuovo - The so called Theodoric's Palace - S. Maria in Porto (in the centre of the city) - The Loggia Lombardesca.

5) St. Apollinare in Classe - The excavations of a Basilica 1 mile south of St. Apollinare - The excavations of S. Severo - Mausoleum of Theodoric.

HISTORICAL SURVEY

Today a wide expanse of well cultivated land encircles Ravenna, but in ancient times the city, which arose upon a group of sand-hills, was washed by the sea and surrounded by marshes. The group of small islands on which the early centre of the city was built was, however, not entirely isolated, for, north and south, it was connected with that chain of dunes which extended to the delta of the river Po on one side, and on the other to the environs of Cervia.

This long chain of sand-dunes at those times formed a barrier against the sea, but with the passing of the centuries, and the accumulation of alluvial deposits brought down by the various branches of the Po, a new crescent of dunes, marking the limit of the foreshore grew up further eastward, starting from Classe and extending northward.

During the Middle Ages and the centuries that followed the low-lying areas were gradually filled up, so that the sea receded more and more, and the seashore is now nearly 4½ miles from the city.

* * *

The early history of Ravenna is lost in the mists of time. Dioniges of Halicarnassus says that the city was founded seven generations before the Trojan War, but we cannot really be sure of this, nor do we know anything of the earliest inhabitants, though Strabo considers that they were of Hellenic descent and had come from Thessaly.

Plan of the ancient town of Ravenna, by M.V. Coronelli (end of XVIIth century.)

In historic times the city was perhaps inhabited, or rather occupied, for a short period by the Etruscans. This might be deduced not only from the fact that Strabo states that the Thessalonians had to abandon the city as a result of Etruscan attacks, and that they called in the Umbrians before returning to their homes, but more especially from the fact that the suffix « -enna » seems to be typically Etruscan.

Further evidence of the temporary presence of Etruscans in the city might be assumed from the circumstance that some objects undoubtedly of Etruscan make have been found in Ravenna, for example, some small votive bronzes and a fine statuette of a warrior with an Etruscan inscription, belonging perhaps to the 6th century B.C., now preserved in the Museum of Antiquities at Leyden. But it is obvious that such evidence has no definite value, consisting as it does in small portable objects, for these articles may have been used for purposes of exchange, or may have been imported.

In any case the supposition that Ravenna was once inhabited by Etruscans finds no confirmation in historical tradition, which does, however, lay some stress upon the Umbrians, who, as is well known, pushed their way in historical times from Rimini to the banks of the Po.

We do not know exactly when Rome took possession of the city. It is however certain that after the conquest of the Po Valley by the Romans, Ravenna — which had long been a flourishing centre of commerce — was a strategic bulwark of great importance because of its extraordinary geographical position which made it almost impregnable, for it was on one side separated from the inland regions by the marshes, which constituted and excellent defence, while being at the same time in immediate contact with the open sea whence it could easily receive reinforcements and supplies.

It is quite possible that Ravenna's first strong urge to maritime development was due to Marius, for Plutarch tells us that the people of Ravenna erected a marble statue of him in his honour. In any case it seems certain that the first Roman fleet to appear at Ravenna was that of Metellus, Sulla's Legate, who disembarked there in 82 B.C.

Two documents of the end of the 12th century mention also a port of Caius Julius Caesar; but it is obvious that the absence of any earlier evidence does not justify (as Torre has rightly observed) any definite statement or conjecture of any kind on this matter. Yet it is probable that Caesar, who chose Ravenna as his headquarters while treating with the Senate, had, for military reasons, actually carried out some work at the port.

The great development and extension of the port was the work of the Emperor Augustus, who, the better to defend the Adriatic and the seas of the near East, decided to make it the base of a pretorian fleet consisting—so Dion Cassius tells us— of 250 ships.

Thus about 2½ miles to the south-east of Ravenna arose the Port of Classe, whose vast basin was hollowed out at the very place where the most recently formed range of sand-dunes had become separated from the more ancient chain along the shore.

But the work carried out in Ravenna by the founder of the Empire was not limited to the construction of a great military port. He planned a wide canal which should unite it with the southern branch of the river Po. This was the « Fossa Augusti » mentioned by several writers. Before reaching Ravenna it seems to have divided into two branches; the one surrounded the city walls the better to assure defence, the other flowed through the midst of the city thus assisting commercial activity.

In the Augustan era commerce was mainly by water, for Strabo says that in his days the city—where the houses were built upon piles—was intersected by many waterways regularly swept by the tides which washed out the muddy pools and so kept the air pure. Thus at that time Ravenna, consisting as it did of various islands linked together by numerous bridges, must have presented an altogether remarkable appearance.

Some idea of it—even if not quite corresponding to the truth—may be derived from a graphic reconstruction attempted towards the end of the 17th century by the noted cosmographer of Ravenna, M. V. Coronelli, who, in another design, based especially on information left us by the Arian Bishop Jordanes, tried to show the neighbouring communities of Caesarea and Classe which had developed enormously as a result of having become the permanent station of the great Roman naval fleet.

From that time too Ravenna became familiar with the activities of the shipyards; there is certain proof of this in a funeral pillar (« stele ») to the « faber navalis » i.e. the carpenter of the fleet, Publius Longidienus, who had caused himself to be shown upon in the act of working with an axe near an unfinished ship. While the city was growing in size as a result of the increasing population, it was, at the same time, being adorned with fine sculptures.

There is the splendid example of the relief to be seen in the National Museum, showing the members of the Julius-Claudian family.

Like other ancient cities Ravenna had a quadrangular perimeter, only the north-east side deviated somewhat from the regularity of the usual plan because of the two waterways all along that side. It is probable also that the nature of the ground did not permit the exact orientation of the « cardo » and the « decumanus » with regard to the four cardinal points. In fact, the two main arteries of the city of Ravenna show an inclination of 45°, one running in the direction SW-NE and the other SE-NW. It is thus not possible to decide with certainty which represented the « cardo » and which the « decumanus ». But as the latter was almost always the wider and more important, it is likely enough that in Ravenna it ran SW-NE for a distance of about 490 yards, i.e. from the «Porta Aurea» to the « Pons Augustus » (Via Salara).

This being the state of affairs, the « cardo » must have been on the SE-NW axis and must have had at its extremities those two gates which at a later time were called respectively « Porta Salustra » and « Porta », or rather « Posterula Latronum ». They opened in the city wall which was built, or at least restored, by the Emperor Claudius in the first year of his reign, 43 A.D.

The « Porta Aurea », on the contrary, certainly owes its origin to Claudius, for an inscription (of which today a few fragments remain) mentions Tiberius Claudius. This gate, which had two openings, was flanked by two round towers. In fact it is shown thus on the mediaeval seal of the city, and in drawings left by some Renaissance

The National Museum - The Roman funeral stele of Publius Longidienus

architects, for example those of Palladio and Sangallo. The two round towers were thrown down by the Venetians at the end of the 15th century and the gate itself was demolished in 1582 merely to supply building material.

Not far from the Porta Aurea stood the Temple of

11

National Museum - Marble patera belonging to «Porta Aurea»

Apollo and the Amphitheatre, but nothing remains of these, nor yet of the Circus and the Capitol, of which the latter stood near the present church of St. Dominic.

At the beginning of the 2nd century the Emperor Trajan provided the city with an aqueduct, for Ravenna, as we learn from Martial, was without drinking water; nor can we be surprised at this when we consider the character of the ground and the nearness of the sea.

So water from the Apennines was brought from the region of Teodorano to Ravenna closely following the

Ronco, and when the course of this river was diverted, a few piles and arches of the ancient aqueduct were found in its bed not far from the church of S. Bartolomeo in Longana, in the year 1735.

As it grew in importance and in the number of its inhabitants Ravenna grew rapidly in size even before the 2nd century A.D. Buildings began to arise outside the « oppidum » as the old municipal centre was called, in the region which was later called « Regio Caesarum ».

But a still greater expansion took place at the beginning of the 5th century when the Emperor Honorius made Ravenna the Capital of the Empire of the West, in place of Milan. The city then soon lost the appearance of a provincial town and assumed the dignity and grandeur of an imperial residence.

Thus, in the new parts which were added to the inhabited area, arose magnificent public buildings and superb churches, the interiors of which were covered with splendid mosaics; such, for example, were the great Ursian Basilica with its five naves and adjoining Baptistery, the Church of Santa Croce and the so-called Mausoleum of Galla Placidia, the Church of St. John the Evangelist, and the church then dedicated to the Apostles, but now to St. Francis.

At the same time the city walls were also extended as a result of the work first of Honorius and Valentinian III, and later by command of Odoacre and Theodoric. With the entrance of Odoacre into Ravenna, and the death of his brother Paul, uncle of Romulus Augustulus, in the pine wood of Classe in 476, the history of the Roman

Empire of the West comes to an end. Odoacre was the first of the barbarians to bear the title of King in Italy.

But towards the last decade of the 5th century, preceded by his fame as a conqueror after victories won in battle on the banks of the Isonzo, at Verona, and on the Adda, Theodoric appeared in the neighbourhood of Ravenna at the head of a mighty host of Ostrogoths. After a siege of almost three years, Theodoric, on March 5th, 493, compelled Odoacre—by this time definitely cut off from all possibility of obtaining reinforcements and supplies—to consent to negotiation. It was promised that his life would be spared, and he was given hope that he might retain part of his authority. But ten days later he was accused of treachery and slain in the Laureto Palace, together with his brother, his wife, and later his son.

Theodoric assumed the title of « Dominus », and later of « Rex », and—as even Procopius assures us—was a wise and enlightened sovereign. He gave a great impulse to building, undertook extensive work for reclaiming land from the surrounding marshes, and restored Trajan's aqueduct; in fact, some leaden « fistulae » or pipes for the conduct of water found in 1938, bear in relief an inscription which reads: « D(omi)n(us) Rex Theodoricus civitati reddidit.

Among the great buildings erected by Theodoric must be mentioned his residence, the « Palatium », and some idea of its exterior appearance—even if only partial—is given by the mosaic showing it at the beginning of the right wall of S. Apollinare Nuovo, but its ground plan

14

is known to us as a result of the excavation carried out by Ghirardini in the early part of this century.

An Arian, and the head of an Arian people, Theodoric wished his subjects to have their own churches. Thus arose the « Anastasis Gothorum », today the Church of Santo Spirito, which served as a Cathedral, and was near the Arian Baptistery. Beside his Palace Theodoric then erected that stupendous Basilica originally dedicated to the Saviour, today called S. Apollinare Nuovo.

In these churches officiated the Arian Bishops, who, following the teaching of Arius, maintained the heretical doctrine (already condemned by the Council of Nicea in 325 and later by the Council of Costantinople in 381) according to which only God the Father is « not begotten », while Christ the Logos is begotten, and he, being different from God, is God by adoption, and not by nature.

In Ravenna there was no violent clash between Arians and Catholics; but some serious conflicts did take place towards the end of Theodoric's reign, for the Sovereign, not satisfied with the results of Pope John's mission (524-525) to the Emperor Justinus in the East and his efforts to obtain favours advantageous to the Arians, kept the Pope a prisoner, and when he died in 526 (little more thant three months before Theodoric) he was considered a martyr—« victima Christi ».

In May 540 Belisarius, Justinian's General, succeeded by means of a stratagem in entering Ravenna where the Goths were resisting under the command of Vitiges. Thus the city passed into the hand of the Byzantines, and in 554 became the seat of the Prefecture of Italy. Shortly after

Justinian issued an edict granting to the Catholics all the real estate belonging to the Arians. The Baptistery was transformed into the Church of S. Maria, and the Church of the Saviour was « reconciled » and dedicated to St. Martin, the Bishop of Tours who had so strenuously opposed the heretics. The principles of St. Basil held by the Catholic Church were vigorously affirmed, and one can catch as it were an echo of this reaffirmation in these words written in the book held by Christ in the mosaic that covered the apse of S. Michele in Africisco (now in the Berlin State Museum) which run: « Ego et Pater unum sumus (I and the Father are One).

A few decades later—as a result of the struggles with the Longobards—power passed into the hands of military governors called Exarchs, who may be almost regarded as Viceroys considering that upon them depended, as Andrea-Agnello—the 9th century historian, author of the « Liber Pontificalis Ecclesiae Ravennatis »—writes, the « regnum et principatum omnis Italiae » (the kingdom and principality of all Italy). In Ravenna the Exarchs, who held civil powers as well as military, established a real court of their own modelled on that of the Emperors.

Just at first the Byzantines brought back into the city all the pomp and ostentation of oriental life, and beautified their buildings with marbles from Proconnesos and mosaics executed by artists trained perhaps at Byzantium.

Sculpture, which had already in the previous century produced works which, for the wide spacing of the figures, was different both from the iconographic point of view and from that of style, from Italic and Gallic sculpture,

16

now takes on a new aspect; one perceives in parapets and capitals contrasts of light and shade determined by the alternation of mass and space; in panels and altar-fronts, in pulpits and in the « pulvini » surmounting capitals, sculpture now adopts a decorative system which finds its typical mode of expression in scantiness of relief and an increased flatness of modelling.

But this splendid artistic impulse lasted only a short time, partly because the great port of Classe, being no longer the station of the fleet, was neglected and fell into disrepair, and lost its original efficiency, becoming in great part silted up. In fact, Jordanes, who was writing about the middle of the 6th century, tells us that where once the ancient port had been he saw not masts with sails but trees bearing fine fruit (« quod aliquando portus fuerit, spatiosissimus hortus ostendit arboribus plenus, verum de quibus non pendent vela sed poma »).

In consequence trade and commerce declined and the city, ill governed for almost two centuries by the Exarchs and then for a brief period about the middle of the 8th century by the Longobards and the Franks, was reduced to the end of its strength, and the efforts of the Archbishops to make the Church of Ravenna independent of Rome, were not enough to maintain the dignity and power of the city.

During the epoch of the Ottos the Archbishops became great feudatories of the Empire, and the city seemed to recover something of its former life.

Thus arose the Comune, among the very earliest in Italy, and it came a « Studio » or University, and a School of a Legal Practice (« Ars notaria »). But power soon fell into the hands of the great families, sometimes Guelf, at others Ghibelline, who carried on their feud, till, in the 13th and 14th centuries, the Da Polenta family gained the upper hand and became rulers of the city. Among the members of this family we may make especial mention of Guido Novello who generously offered hospitality to Dante Alighieri, who had been exiled from Florence and died at Ravenna on September 13th, 1321.

From the beginning of the 15th century Ravenna was under the jurisdiction of the Venetian Republic which exercised direct rule from 1441 to 1509, in which year it passed by treaty to the Church. Three years afterwards the city, defended by the armies of the Holy League, was closely besieged by Louis XII, King of France, who took it by storm and sacked it with fire and sword (April 12th, 1512).

A long period of obscurity followed, and with the French Revolution Ravenna even lost its rank as Capital of Romagna, an honour which was transferred to Forlì.

After being returned to the Church in 1815, it was the seat of the Legation till 1859, and in the following year it was definitely united to the Kingdom of Italy.

ITINERARY N. 1

Piazza del Popolo - The Dante area
S. Francesco
The Town Art Gallery
Sant'Agata Maggiore

*

PIAZZA DEL POPOLO

This large well contained rectangular square marks the centre of the town, not only in its position, but because it has many public buildings overlooking it, for example the Town-Hall and Prefecture.

The oldest and most characteristic part is on the south west, where the Town-Hall forms a corner with the Venetian Palace, and two high columns have stood nearby since 1483.

The Venetians surmounted these columns with statues of St. Apollinare, first Bishop of Ravenna and the Lion of S. Marco.

The latter was substituted by a statue of St. Vitale in 1509. The circular pedestals in the form of steps on which

Piazza del Popolo

P. Lombardi carved elegant decorative motifs, are very characteristic.

The Town Hall was built in 1400 but almost completely rebuilt in 1681, and some of the exterior decoration, such as the window ornaments and heavy battlements were added during the last century. Two very interesting points are to be noted in the rather low but wide porticoes on the lower part and, higher, the round ocular openings above the windows.

The Venetian Palace, erected during the second half of the XV century also has a series of very wide and airy porticoes on the lower part, over which stand beautiful white columned mullioned windows and a small balcony.

It is interesting to note how the granite columns of the porticoes are crowned by capitals decorated with acanthus leaves and on four of them King Theodoric's monogram is carved; they come from the church of St. Andrew of the Goths, which was destroyed by the Venetians during their dominion over the city.

THE DANTE AREA

DANTE'S TOMB - THE FRANCISCAN CLOISTERS - THE GARDENS

Towards the end of Via Dante just at the bottom, rises the Tomb of the Great Poet, who died, in exile at Ravenna, on the night between 13th and 14th September 1321.

The small and modest construction, of a sober neo-classic style, was built in 1780 by C. Morigia at the wishes of the Cardinal Legate, L. Valenti Gonzaga, whose coat-of-arms surmounts the door.

On the wall facing the door on entering, lined with marble is the sepulchre containing Dante's bones. The chest bears a Latin epitaph by B. Canaccio carved in 1327.

The English translation is as follows: « The rights of monarchy, the heavens and infernal lakes of the Phlege-thon that I visited I sang, as long as mortal destiny decreed. But my soul was taken to a better place and reached its creator among the stars. Here I lie buried, Dante, exile from my birth-place, a son of Florence, that loveless mother ».

And above the chest is a golden cross given by Pope Paul VI on the occasion of the seven hundredth anniversary of

Tomb
of Dante

the birth of the poet, and just below is the bas-relief
carved by P. Lombardi in 1483, representing a thought-
ful Dante at a lectern.

At the foot of the chest since 1921 one can see the bronze
wreath placed there by the victorious Italian army of
the first world war. From the middle of the domed ceiling

hangs a small votive lamp, the oil for which comes from the Tuscany hills and is presented on every anniversary by the Florence town council.

Towards the end of the XV century Bernard Bembo, Venetian lord of Ravenna moved Dante's tomb to the western wall of one of the quiet Franciscan cloisters from which the monks by working a hole from the inside of the wall removed the poet's bones in 1519, thus avoiding their transfer to Florence, ordered by the Medici Pope Leone X.

The bones were jealously kept hidden in the Franciscan monastery near the ever-green garden of the Braccio-forte quadrangle, until 1865 when they were found. Under the arches of « Braccioforte » the ex-oratorium, there are two very antique marble sarcophagi. One of these, of the V century, is very interesting with its four carved panels, which were described by G. D'Annunzio in his « Francesca da Rimini ».

The redeemer
Has a lion and a serpent under foot;
Elizabeth visits Mary;
The angel appears to the blessed Virgin;
Deer quenching their thirst at a spring.

Interior of the Tomb of Dante

Basilica of St. Francesco

THE CHURCH OF S. FRANCESCO

(Piazza S. Francesco)

The church of S. Francesco rises at the far end of a quiet square, bordered on its southern side by the Provincial Administration Offices and on the north by XVI century porches (formerly belonging to the monastery of Porto) and put here in 1936. The church was built during the last half of the V century by Bishop Neone and was dedicated to St. Peter and St. Paul.

Nothing remains today of this construction, as the whole church was rebuilt in the X and XI centuries. A little earlier than this, the rectangular bell-tower with two, three and four mullioned windows was added. Entrusted to the Franciscan monks in 1261, it was given the name of S. Francesco; and it is here that in 1321 the funeral of Dante was held, whose body (as Boccaccio writes) was encased in a « stone chest » and placed in the portico, which was destroyed some centuries ago.

The inside of the church is divided into three aisles with two rows of antique marble columns and covered by a medieval wooden ceiling representing the reversed keel of a ship. It is striking for its simplicity and harmony of line and draws the visitors' eye to the apse under which a raised presbytery covers the crypt and oratory, built a little before the year 1000 A.D. and visible through small openings. The crypt is constantly under water. The pavement of the crypt is that of the original V century construction with its mosaics, and one can see the Latin inscription referring to the burial of the founder, Archbishop Neone.

Two really beautiful antique marble sarcophagi considered by some to be about the last half of the IV century or the first half of the V, are conserved inside the church. One, partly restored, supports the high altar, the other is to be found about half way along the left hand aisle.

Both of these belong to the type called «a colonne» because their side niches are divided by columns, between which there are figures of Christ and the Apostles.

Basilica of St. Francesco - Interior

THE CHURCH OF SANT'AGATA MAGGIORE

(Via Mazzini)

The foundation of this church goes back to the end of the V century. Behind a « quadroportico » the traces of which were ascertained during the excavations of 1913-19, and flanked by a cylindrical bell-tower of the late medieval period, the church (49.50 x 25 m) is divided into three aisles by two rows of ten columns each, which, together with the pavement are higher than the original elevation of 2.80 m.

During the recent restorations the apse windows have been re-opened, and here traces of the old mosaic decoration can be found. The higher part of the apse, which was built of the typical brick used in the buildings of Argentarius, goes back to about the middle of the VI century; as were the mosaics of the absidal cupola according to remaining designs.

These mosaics represented the Enthroned Christ between two Arcangels and were completely destroyed by a violent earthquake in 1688. Various sarcophagi and marble fragments are conserved in the church; noteworthy is the very fine VI century panel that takes the place of the high-altar.

ITINERARY N. 2

The Cathedral
The Cathedral Baptistry or Neone Baptistry
The Archiepiscopal Museum
The Archiepiscopal Chapel

*

THE CATHEDRAL

(Piazza Duomo)

The antique cathedral of Ravenna was, from the time it was built, the beginning of the V century, commonly called after its founder Archbishop Ursus, « Basilica Ursiana ». As this building was more or less a ruin by 1734 it was completely demolished to give place to the actual construction. Instead of five aisles the architect G. Buonamici of Rimini rebuilt it with three.

At the intersection of the vaults a dome was built that the original building did not possess and at the two ends chapels were added, the left hand one built according to the plans of C. Moderno and called the chapel of the Holy Sacrament, containing frescoes by C. Reni and some of his disciples. The right hand chapel of the « Madonna del Sudore » was decorated by Giambattista and Andrea

The Ortodox Baptistery

interior (5th cent.)

Dome

Barbiani. Inside this chapel are the two most monumental paleochristian sarcophagi in Ravenna, both with semi-cylindrical covers.

The left hand one, goes back to the first half of the V century, and was used to deposit the remains of Archbishop Rinaldo da Concorreggio who died in 1321. On the front panel is an Enthroned Christ above the mount with the sources of the four symbolic rivers of Paradise, who welcomes the two apostles St. Peter and St. Paul, as the two Saints advance offering crowns in their veiled hands. On each side of the Saints are two large palm trees.

Into the right hand sarcophagus, which can be dated to a little before the middle of the V century, in 1658 were transferred the ashes of S. Barbaziano, councillor of Galla Placidia.

On the front of this too, appear the figures of Christ, and the apostles Peter and Paul. They are shown full faced in stiff attitudes, but, this time, inside niches with shell ornamentation.

A third sarcophagus, also of the first half of the V century, is preserved in the church. It supports an altar placed about half way up the right hand nave. On it, between two palms are the figures of Christ and the two apostles, and in 1809 the remains of Archbishop Esuperanzio and Massimiano were deposited in it. Along the right hand side of the middle aisle, about half way, in 1913 the marble ambo in the shape of a tower, was re-constructed. This ambo was donated to the Cathedral by Archbishop Agnello (557-570) as can be seen from the inscription

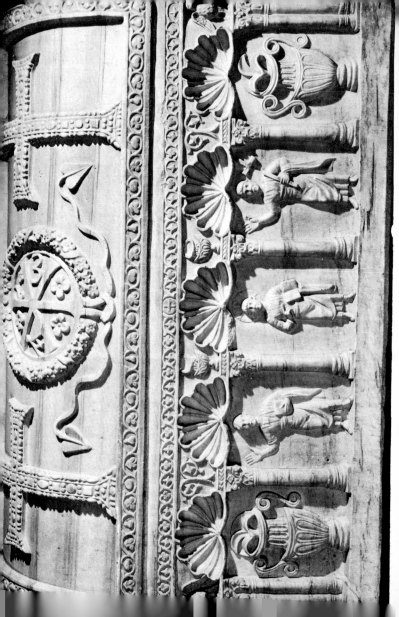

The Cathedral · The pulpit erected by Bishop Agnellus

39

running along the crowning frame. The decoration consists of a series of bands, divided into squares containing repeated flat figures of fish, ducks, doves, deer, peacocks and lambs. Outside, on the left hand side of the Cathedral rises the cylindrical (35 m) bell-tower, the oldest documentation of which goes back to the year 1038.

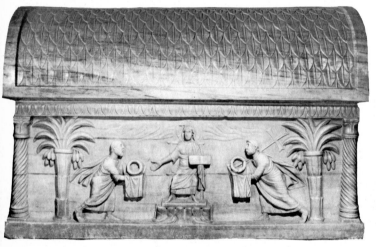

The Cathedral · Sarcophagus of Archbishop Rinaldo da Concorreggio

The Cathedral

The Cathedral - Fresco by G. Reni

NEONE BAPTISTRY

(Via Battistero)

Erected by Archbishop Ursus at the beginning of the V century and adjoining the cathedral, this baptistry like the one adjoining the cathedral in Milan goes back to the IV century, and is also octagonal. Its original level is about nine feet below street level. Originally each of the four flat sides, alternating with four apses, contained a door. To-day only the archway above each is visible.

In the beginning of the second half of the V century Archbishop Neone built a dome over the building and, as the historian A. Agnello, testifies, covered it with magnificent mosaics, still existing today. If the outside of the baptistry shows, on the upper parts pensil arches — and this structure shows clearly a later rebuilding — the inside shows a well calculated series of vertical shiny multicoloured marble marquetries, stuccoes and mosaics, so that architecture and decoration become a single harmonious whole.

Baptistry of the Cathedral - Baptism of Jesus (5th cent.)

The domed roof, constructed with small terracotta tubes to save weight, is completely covered with mosaic decoration which can be divided into three zones, viz: the centre and two concentric zones. In the circle at the very centre of the dome is the Baptism of Christ. Here Christ is shown standing in the waters of the Jordan while St. John goes through the baptist rites and a symbolic personification of the river itself (an old man) emerges to offer the Saviour a green garment to dry Him, (the dove, Christ's head and the right arm of St. John are 18th century restorations).

In the second zone (from centre) on an indigo background and separated by thin floral stanchions in golden mosaic, are the twelve apostles in two formations led respectively by St. Peter and St. Paul. The apostles are shown walking slowly, holding symbolic jewelled crowns in their covered hands. The apostles may be identified by the name written by the side of each head. The outside ring contains eight architectural sections, each curving into an apse at the centre: in each of these there is a throne and an altar, alternately, alluding to the majesty and divinity of Christ. The thrones are between two « viridaria » symbol of the celestial gardens, surrounded by transennae; the trees are flanked by two empty seats; alluding to those prepared by Christ, for the Elect. Next a little lower at the height of the windows, are the stucco decorations and figures of the prophets in niches. These motifs, like the mosaics, are of the same period,

Baptistry of the
Cathedral ·
Marble Roman vase

as Archbishop Neone, (451-475 A.D.). Lower still, within
a ring or round there is a mosaic (much restored) among
green acanthus sprays sparkling with gold on the dark
blue background. By observing the domed roof as a whole,
one sees how the general idea is of a great spoked wheel,
rotating around a fixed central nucleus, represented in this
case by the centre « medallion ». Because of the tremen-
dous centrifugal force caused by this effect the decorations suggest the idea of the continuous and infinite.

ARCHIEPISCOPAL MUSEUM

The Archiepiscopal Museum is situated on the first floor of the Archiepiscopal Palace: the material collected there comes above all from the old Cathedral "Ursiana" which was destroyed in the XVIII century. The mosaic fragments here come from the apsidal motif of the church and show the Virgin Mary at prayer and the heads of St. John, the Evangelist, St. Peter, S. Barbazian, S. Ursicino and a soldier, and are fixed to the wall of the first room. Below these fragments are the marble transennae probably of the VI cent.

On the opposite wall, in the centre, is a part of the marble ambo from the church of St. John and St. Paul, which is characterized by a series of panels forming diverse overlapping folds each of which surrounds the figure of an extremely flat animal. The inscription running along the top frame is considered to be of the Marinian episcopacy, towards the end of the VI cent.

In the first room there are some capitals, considered by some to be of the VI century, and by others, of the V. These capitals are decorated with animal-forms. Very notable is the small rectangular marble « capsella », of

SCA MARIA

XIIth century mosaic from the Cathedral

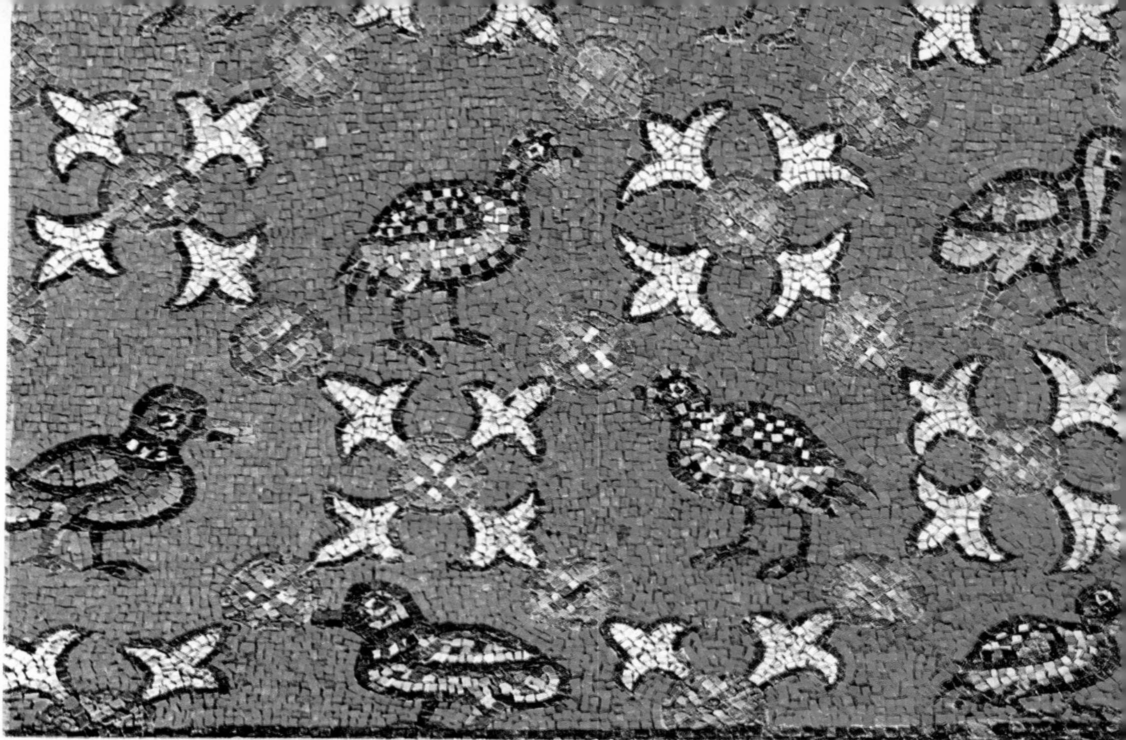

Archiepiscopal museum - Vault

the V century. Its four sides show the following: Daniel in the lions' den, the adoration of the kings, the women at the Tomb, the Ascension, and lastly the delivering of the Commandments. Under the entrance archway of the second room, in 1961, a Greek marble sarcophagus was placed. This sarcophagus, was for two hundred years enclosed in the high altar of the Cathedral. The sarcophagus belongs to the end of the V century or beginning of the VI and is of the type called « columned » because each of its four sides contain a series of niches, the whole crowned by shells and supported by columns. The remaining walls of the room contain Christian funeral inscriptions in Latin, the oldest found in Ravenna.

In the centre of the second room on the walls of which some Roman epigraphs and bas-reliefs may be seen there is a beautiful porphyry statue. Unfortunately the head was missing when it was found. It is of an Emperor of the late imperial age in the act of replacing his sword into its scabbard.

In some of the cases at the far end of a corridor some very interesting pieces of material are kept. More noteworthy than the purple coloured veil and the VII-VIII century fragments of episcopal girdles, found in 1940 in a sarcophagus in the right hand apse of St. Apollinaris in Classe, is the great chasuble called « Angelopte » of the last half of the XII century.

This very fine chasuble is in dark-blue coloured brocade and adorned with quarter moons and small eagles. In a small circular adjoining room there is the rarest relic in the museum: the famous ivory throne of Archbishop

The archiepiscopal museum: ivory chair of S. Massimiano (detail)

Maximian who was archbishop of Ravenna towards the end of the first half of the VI century. It is thought that this throne was probably donated by the Emperor Justinian himself.

On the front panel among the decorative motifs, are the four Evangelists and John the Baptist, on the back are scenes from the life of Jesus, some of which are inspired by the canonical texts. On the rear panels are episodes from the life of Joseph.

The scholars are divided about the origins of this masterpiece of carving, which clearly shows the hands of different artists; some think it was carved at Alexandria, others at Constantinople and some even think it was carved in Ravenna itself.

The archiepiscopal museum: Marble chest with the scene of the Magi offering their gifts

53

Archiepiscopal Chapel - Jesus Christ as a soldier

Archiepiscopal Chapel: interior of the oratory

THE ARCHIEPISCOPAL CHAPEL

or ORATORY OF S. ANDREA

(Piazza Arcivescovado, 1)

To reach the chapel one crosses the rooms of the Episcopal Museum. This chapel was erected by a certain Archbishop Peter: but probably it isn't Peter I or III (570-578),
as was until recently thought, but Peter II who was archbishop from 494 to 519, thus in the full Theodorian period.

The chapel is behind a small rectangular atrium bearing on its walls painted imitations of mosaics. Some traces
of the original still remain and are described in twenty
Latin hexameters thanks to the transcription of the historian A. Agnello in the IX century. The first of these
is very significant because it underlines poetically the light
given out by the mosaics: **Aut lux hic nata est capta hic
libera regnat** (« light is born here, or made prisoner and
here reigns freely »).

Over the door is the figure of the Warrior Christ: the
bottom half is a complete restoration but was traced on
a secure base, showing Christ's head with a halo and cross
dressed in armour and cloak. He appears full faced in
the act of trampling on the neck of a lion and a serpent,
symbols of the powers of evil. In his right hand he is
holding a long cross resting on his shoulder, and in his left
an open book, on the pages of which can be seen the
words he spoke describing himself: **Ego sum via, veritas
et vita** (I am the way, truth and life).

The Archiepiscopal museum · G. Boni da Mantova · Crib, 1493

IACO BVS

IOHA NNES

Archi-
episcopal
Chapel -
detail

The Oratory itself, in the form of a cross, ends in a small apse, the dome of which, now completely painted in tempera, represents the sky at night with a cross in the centre. The dome is gold with the monogram of Christ, formed by the intertwined Greek letters, I (iota) and ϰ

PAVLVS

ACO BVS

Archiepiscopal Chapel - The Apostle St. Paul

Archiepiscopal Chapel - The Apostle St. Peter

(chi) signifying Jesus Christ. This monogram is shown supported by four angels lined along the rib-structure of the vault ceiling itself.

Between the angels supporting the monogram are the four winged symbols of the Evangelists emerging from coloured clouds, the Eagle (St. John), Man (St. Matthew), the Calf (St. Luke), the Lion (St. Mark). Under the eastern and western archways, within circular medallions are busts of the apostles on each side of the bust of Christ; under the northern and southern archways are the busts of six male and six female saints (the former partly restored).

The six female saints with gems in their hair and around their necks are embellished by a white silk veil, adorned with precious stones which from their heads, falls over and behind their shoulders. In the chapel one may see the precious silver cross called « Agnello cross » after the archbishop who had it made for him during his episcopacy, between 557 and 570 A.D.

All the four arms of the cross, are decorated with circular medallions containing busts of the saints. Some of these were restored in the XVI century, especially the ones on the lower arm. The medallions containing the Virgin Praying, on one side, and the Resurrection on the other, at the highest point of the cross, were done about this period.

ITINERARY N. 3

The Mausoleum of Galla Placidia
S. Vitale
The National Museum

*

THE MAUSOLEUM OF GALLA PLACIDIA

The august Galla Placidia, daughter of Teodosio II, and first wife of Atawulf and then of Constance III, after the death of his brother Emperor Honorius in 423 A.D., reigned in lieu of her son Valentinian III who was still a boy, and moved from Constantinople, where they lived, to Ravenna. Galla Placidia was a woman of great firmness, but of singular piety, and built various new churches

Mausoleum of Galla Placidia

here among which was the cruciform or cross-shaped church of St. Croce.

At the far end of the narthex of this she built two small constructions also cruciform. Of these, the right hand one, called the « Mausoleum of Galla Placidia », still remains today structurally complete and isolated. This was due to the transformation of the church after the

64

The so-called Mausoleum of Galla Placidia -
Detail of the mosaics of the vault (5th cent.)

The so-called Mausoleum of Galla Placidia · Detail of the decoration (5th cent.)

demolition of the lateral wing and its narthex, and the shortening of the front (to make way for a road at that point). Of the exact opposite construction which has disappeared, on the left at the far end of the narthex, scholar Cortesi, by using hand drilling in 1967 discovered traces of the foundations.

According to medieval tradition the remaining cruciform building, (measuring 12 m 75 cm x 10 m 25 cm) was used as a burial place for the Empress, but modern historians disagree with this, as G. Placidia who died in 450 A.D. in Rome, should have been buried in the Theodosian family tomb in St. Peter's. We know that a few months before she died she had her father's remains transferred there from Constantinople. It is probable that the building in Ravenna was intended as an Imperial Mausoleum by the pious Empress, but it is difficult to know who **de facto** was actually buried there.

Due to the slow but constant subsiding of the ground of Ravenna (about 1 m 50 cm, five feet) the Mausoleum today is lower and, as it is not so high as it was, doesn't appear in its original proportions. Like the other antique religious buildings in Ravenna the architectural form of this « sacellum » (about the second quarter of the V century A.D.) presents an external simplicity. Except for the facade, which formed the southern extremity of the narthex of the church of S. Croce, this little building is rhythmically decorated on each side by a series of blind arches which serve to embellish the whole.

At the intersection of the vaults there is a small square tower which internally is dome-shaped. The extreme external simplicity of the sacellum certainly gives no clue to the matchless sumptuousness of the internal decoration. Over a high yellow marble border (rebuilt between 1898 and 1902) there is the mosaic decoration covering the walls and ceiling, perfectly adapted to the architecture, and on the whole beautifully preserved. The chromatic range, using an intense indigo blue as a back-ground, changes to the harmonious tones of grey-white, gold and light blues, brightened with sober touches of reds, greens and yellows, thus creating a delicate and subdued atmosphere and bringing a sense of wonder and enchantment to the visitor. The filtered light coming from the alabaster windows is warm and golden coloured. The domed-ceiling, above the four winged Evangelistic symbols emerging from thin coloured clouds; viz: the Lion (St. Mark), the Eagle (St. John), the Calf (St. Luke), and Man (St. Matthew), shows a night sky with 570 golden stars rotating concentrically around a golden Latin cross, symbol of redemption, occupying the very centre of the dome.

In the four lunettes on each side of the dome, with a decorative motif running around them, and under great shell shaped forms are 8 white figures of Apostles in acts of adoration. Among these, on the eastern lunette we recognize St. Peter holding a key in his left hand, and St. Paul. The other four Apostles are to be found two on

The so-called Mausoleum of Galla Placidia - Drinking pidgeons (VI cent.)

each side of the lateral vault on elegant stanchions, amidst a luxurious intertwining of vines.

The lunettes at the bottom of each short transept present the same thematic composition: a small lake surrounded by grass and two deer about to slake their thirst, all this in the midst of a symmetrical pattern of swirling acanthus. This scene is clearly symbolical, because it brings to mind a line from psalm XLI - 1-2: « As deer need the spring, so, O Lord, my soul needs you ». The ceilings of the four transepts are covered by a mosaic that gives the impression of a soft indigo coloured oriental carpet, on which red and white flower calyxes and golden globes shine.

On the lunette directly in front of the entrance door is St. Lawrence carrying the book of Psalms and a cross with the emblem of his supposed martyrdom, the flaming gridiron. Near the gridiron is a chest with the four red books of the apostles. Above each is the name of the author. In the lunette over the entrance door is the charming mosaic figure of the « Good Shepherd and his flock »; Jesus in a golden tunic and purple mantle, his head surrounded by a great halo occupies the centre of the scene, seated almost full-face on a rock.

The so-called Mausoleum of Galla Placidia - St. Laurence's martyrdom

With his left hand he supports a tall cross and is in the act of beckoning one of the six sheep to his side. All the sheep are turned towards Christ, and the whole scene takes place in a rural landscape of trees and fields immersed in a soft morning light gradually becoming the pale blue of the far horizon. The most singular thing here is the wonderful figure of Christ who, by the position of his face and right arm, concentrates the movement of the scene upon himself.

The so-called Mausoleum of Galla Placidia -
The sorcophagus called that of Costantius III

The so-called Mausoleum of Galla Placidia - Lunette with the Good Shepherd (5th cent.)

At the present day there are three marble Sarcophagi inside the mausoleum, all three typical examples of Ravenna art.

The one under the image of St. Lawrence is the biggest and has a double shaped top and angular acroteria. In the centre of the front and back of this there is a rectangular space without inscription: this is the sarcophagus that is commonly called «Galla Placidia's». The late V century sarcophagus, in the left transept, is considered to be of Galla Placidia's second husband Costanzo III. On the front of this sarcophagus, in the centre, is the mystic lamb on the mount from which the four symbolical rivers of Paradise spring, between two lambs, representing the Apostles, and two palm-trees, symbol of the Justice.

The early VI century sarcophagus in the right transept, said to be of Valentinian III, son of G. Placidia has a semicircular top with a fish scale design covering it. Its front contains three panels each containing a cross: the middle panel has two doves carved on the arms of the cross and the mystic Lamb on the mount. The same scene is shown on the corresponding rear panels, but in this case, unfinished.

The so-called Mausoleum of Galla Placidia - Interior (5th cent.)

THE BASILICA OF S. VITALE

The Ravenna historian Andrea-Agnello, of the IX century speaking of S. Vitale, said that no other temple in Italy could be compared with it. In fact the architecture of S. Vitale appears prodigious because it embraces the whole range of technical knowledge, regarding construction and stability, and the structural forms used, and lastly the splendour of the decorative elements.

S. Vitale - Throne of Neptune (detail)

The church was begun after 526 A.D. by Archbishop
Ecclesius when Ravenna was still under the dominion of
the Goths, and was financed by the 26,000 pieces of gold
of Giulianus Argentarius, who was, without a doubt not
the architect of the building, as some scholars have said,
but must be considered just a simple, even if very rich,
private banker. But the fact that Emperor Justinian may
have entrusted him with a secret diplomatic mission destined to prepare the way for the Byzantine conquest of
Ravenna, cannot be ruled out.

S. Vitale: Detail from the vault of the Presbytery (VI century)

The building itself was finished in the Spring of 547 A.D., or at the latest 548 A.D.. The construction, carried out in long thin bricks called « Giulianei » (because for the most part they came from the kilns belonging to G. Argentarius), is concentrical. It is built on an octagonal plan which on the outside is divided into two principal parts, the highest, covering the internal dome, shows its clear geometric articulation in its smooth walls, in the centre of each of which is an arched window. The lower part is a little more elaborate.

There are two rows of windows, separated by a small saw-tooth designed cornice. This externally marks the internal division of the perimetral gallery into two floors. Along each side, alternating with the windows, two completely smooth pillaster strips rise to the roof of the building, and together with the buttresses corresponding to each angle, are not only used as reinforcing elements, but as decoration.

Owing to this arrangement the two sides where the old rectangular entrance was situated cannot be seen, but may be noted from the second cloister of the nearby museum or from the side where the apse opens. The latter, semi-hexagonal in shape has two small niches and two circular vestries on its sides; so quite an interesting play of volumes and architectural rhythm is created here.

Entering the very suggestive interior of the church one is immediately struck by the 8 robust columns which draw the eye up to the matroneum or women's gallery, where they continue up to support the central domed ceiling. This dome, is now decorated by frescoes carried out at

S. Vitale - The mosaic decoration on the South wall of the choir

the end of the XVIII century by S. Barozzi, U. Gandolfi, and G. Guarana. The dome is singular in its construction as it was built with a double series, in ever smaller circles, of small terracotta tubes, each fitting into the next.

S. Vitale - The Apse's Niche (detail)

S. Vitale · Detail of the mosaic of the apse

S. Vitale - Mosaics of the choir (detail)

IEREMIA

MOSE

S. Vitale - Detail of the Presbytery

In this way the weight of the dome, compared with its size, is relatively light; so that the pressure on the supporting walls is reduced. The high columns, joined together by open exedrae, divided into two levels and surmounted by triple arches, separate the central space from the somewhat obscure circular ambulatory. In this latter a very picturesque effect is obtained, and, is emphazised even more by the concavity of the exedrae.

These exedrae, being open-worked and therefore almost volumeless, show, in virtue of their atmospheric value, a clear tendency to spread and increase the feeling of space. Thus a lively alternation of space and volume, light and shade is obtained in this way. This play of mass and volume and architectural line seems to point to the deep space of the tribune, in search of a restful interval, where the mosaic decoration begins and where the stuccoes, marbles, the pulvini, the open-worked capitals, and the marble marquetry of the apse, all in harmony with each other and with the general symphonic complex of colours are to be seen.

The cross shaped vault ceiling of the presbytery with a very high curve, and with the mystic lamb in the very centre, has a starry sky for a background.

Four rich festoons of fruit leaves and the arms of four angels reach the centre along the ascending lines of the vault. The four supporting angels are in the centre of each

S. Vitale - Empress Theodora with her Court

S. Vitale · Interior (detail)

gore (or segment) of the vault. These angels are adorned with green acanthus garlands, and the gore itself with a great variety of animals.

On each side of the ample three mullioned windows there is a rocky landscape with lakes and animals, and, among all this are the four Evangelists with their symbol above them. Lower down, in the great lunette of the left wall are two episodes from the life of Abraham; the hospitality shown to the three angels announcing the coming of their son Isaac after he and his wife Sara had waited so long. Then the sacrifice, by divine command, of his son, then the hand of God, coming from the sky to impede Abraham's sword from falling on to the helpless Isaac.

In the right hand lunette on each side of a covered altar, the sacrifice of Abel is shown. Abel is seen dressed in animal skins and offering a lamb for sacrifice. In the same scene we see Melchisedec, the Priest King, and David wearing pontifical garments, and holding a loaf of bread on high. Higher, on each side of the first lunette we can see Moses receiving the Ten Commandments on Mount Sinai, and near the second, Moses about to unfasten his sandles and walk into the burning bush.

The mosaics in the presbytery are distinguishable for the narrative fluency and naturalism and scenes of life they contain: surrounding each figure, in various positions, there is the ever-present landscape; vibrating with atmosphere. The mosaics in the apse are different, the figures are rigidly frontal and are shown on a golden background, full of supreme idealism. In the dome of the apse are the figures of the purple-clad, young and clean-shaven Christ, seated on a blue sphere, symbol of creation, and two archangels, His celestial guards, by His side.

On the left is the Martyr S. Vitale, to whom the church is dedicated, about to receive into his veiled hands the crown of eternal glory from Christ. On the right we see Archbishop Ecclesius, founder of the church, in the act of presenting a model of the Basilica to Christ. This theophanic scene is echoed lower down, in the two famous panels on opposite sides of the apse. They show two scenes of the imperial offering of liturgical vestments to the church, the Emperor Justinian offering the patern or plate and the Empress offering a chalice to be used in Holy Sacrifice.

The Emperor is preceded by the clergy and followed by

S. Vitale - Sarcophagus of Isaacius

S. Vitale - The Emperor Justinian (6th cent.)

S. Vitale - Empress Theodora (6th cent.)

nobles and soldiers. Among these there is Archbishop Maximilian the only one who has his name written over his head. He is shown frontally with a halo, symbolical of the power received from God.

The Empress is preceded by two ministers and followed by her aristocratic looking ladies-in-waiting, dressed in very sumptuous and splendid silk mantles and wearing much jewelry. Her purple cloak bears a gold embroidered offering of the three kings. It is here, above all, in these two panels in the apse that the S. Vitale mosaics show their fascinating movement, rhythm, and exaltation of colour; by contemplating these two examples it is easy to conjure up the splendour of the old Byzantine court.

THE NATIONAL MUSEUM

(Via S. Vitale, 17)

At the left side of the lawn in front of S. Vitale is a very beautiful doorway, which is the entrance to the National Museum. The Museum has been housed in the cloisters of the ex-Monastery since 1913-14. In 1959 fragments and monumental carving of an epigraphical character for the most part were fixed to the walls of the first cloister. The Latin inscriptions mostly concern the « classiarii » or the sailors of the Roman fleet in Classe, the famous port of Ravenna.

These inscriptions not only tell us the name of the sailors, or where they came from, but their age, their service record, promotions and the name and type of ship on which they were embarked. Among the funeral « stele » some of which contain several carved portraits, the I century one of Publius Longidieno, shown finishing the construction of a ship, is, perhaps the most interesting. The bas-relief, commonly called « Apoteosi di Augusto » of the first century is very important. It shows members of the Julius-Claudia family, among which are Augustus and Livia.

On the left of this carving, there is a small room containing all the architectonic-decorative material that has been found, of the « Porta Aurea (one of the city gates), which was opened in 43 A.D. by the Emperor Claudius, and was sacked and dismantled by the Venetians in 1582.

The second cloister (with double pillars) was planned by Andrea Da Valle, and was built in 1562. Here Roman, Paleochristian, Byzantine, Norman, Gothic, Renaissance and Baroque carvings and architectural remains are kept.

Among the many interesting pieces is the sarcophagus of the IV century, the so called « **Traditio Legis** » and a number of VI century capitals decorated with acanthus leaves. These came from an old church of Theodoric; one of these carries the Gothic king's monogram « **Theodericus rex** ».

On the northern side of the second cloister is the doorway leading to a great hall (the ex-refectory of the monastery). In 1965 a VI century mosaic from the church of S. Severo in Classe was placed in the centre of the

National Museum · Roman Sarcophagus

The National Museum · The so-called Apotheosis of Augustus (detail)

floor. On the shorter walls are the 14th century frescoes removed from the apsidal vault of the church of S. Chiara and a great canvas by Luca Longhi, recently restored, and showing a scene from the Last Supper.

In a nearby room there are the archeological relics (funeral stele, glass, and urns etc.) coming from a I century A.D. necropolis discovered in 1966 along the Via Romea Vecchia.

In other rooms nearby, which were originally the old stables, there are floor mosaics. These were recently found on the site of the Church of S. Severo (end of VI century), and perhaps of S. Demetrio, which was discovered 2 kms. south of S. Apollinare in Classe.

In the centre of the third cloister built at the end of the XVIII century, stands the bronze statue of Pope Alexander VII (Chigi), donated by the Ravennate Cardinal

The National Museum - Relief with Hercules and deer (5th cent.)

Rasponi. The upstairs rooms are reached by a XVIII century staircase designed by Benedetto Fiandrini, between the first and second cloister.

In these fifteen rooms are the collections of bronzes, marbles, glass, coins and medals, icons, rare materials, arms, ivory carvings and ceramics. There are a number of extremely interesting marble hermae of Greek personalities found between 1936 and 1938 in the Adriatic sea, about four miles from the shore, and VI century open worked transennae, coming from the church of St. Vitale.

Here you will find the bronze cross, which until 1911, was on the highest point of St. Vitale. Among the very precious materials, there is the IX century piece of sasanide type cloth with a lion design: it was found in the tomb of S. Giuliano in Rimini. There are many interesting ivory pieces, from about the VI century A.D. and the very fine ivory tablet of Coptic art, showing Apollo and Daphne, and the dyptich of Murano, of Egyptian origin. Among the ceramics, very excellent examples from the kilns of Deruta, Faenza, Urbino, and Castelli are not lacking.

The National Museum - Thediptych of Murano (Ivory - 6th cent.)

ITINERARY N. 4

Church of the Spirito Santo
Arian Baptistry
St. John the Evangelist
S. Apollinare Nuovo
The so called palace of Theodoric
S. Maria in Porto - Loggia Lombardesca

*

CHURCH OF THE SPIRITO SANTO (HOLY GHOST)

(Piazzetta degli Ariani)

With this church, probably the first church built by Theodoric after his conquest of Ravenna in 493 A.D., the king wanted to give his people, who were Arian, a church distinct from the Catholics, and dedicated it to the Resurrection. In 561 A.D. once the Goths had been driven from the city, the church was consacrated to S. Teodoro the martyr of Amasea, and reconciled to the Catholic cult.

The Church of Spirito Santo

Only later was it re-named, the Spirito Santo. Apart from the difference between the actual and original height of the pavement and columns (1 m 82 cm.), the interior of the church, which is very luminous, can be said to preserve its original architectural features.

It is divided by two lines of seven columns each, into three naves, and being 26 m 41 cm. long and 16 m 99 cm wide, has thus only limited depth. Under this aspect it brings to mind the proportions of another Arian church, in Rome (built 25 years before): S. Andrea dei Goti. The marble ambo about half way along the pillars on the right is of the Theodoric period.

The lacunar ceiling of the centre nave hiding the former trusses was constructed before the end of the first half of the XVI century, and is of the same period as the small archway in front of the facade. At the bottom of the right hand nave is a large canvas of the Forlivese painter Livio Agresti, showing the « **Dove Bishops** » so called because their election was thought to be due to the appearance of the Dove representing the Holy Ghost.

ARIAN BAPTISTRY

(Piazzetta degli Ariani)

Just by the ex-Arian Cathedral is the baptistry, now sunken about 2 m 25 cm. into the ground. This is the baptistry that Theodoric built about the end of the V century A.D.

Like the Catholic baptistry this too is octagonal in shape, and has four small apses on alternating walls. Originally the construction was surrounded on seven sides by an ambulatory. The actual protective railing shows part of the perimeter. About 750 A.D., the Emperor Justinian gave the Arian churches to the Catholics so this baptistry ceased to be used as such and was therefore transformed into a church, « S. Maria in Cosmedin ». The mosaics on the brick domed ceiling are a simplified version of the Catholic Baptistry, since the central medallion here is surrounded by one concentric strip not two.

The central medallion shows the Baptism of Christ. Here Christ is shown half immersed in the waters of the Jordan, and with John's right hand placed upon his head in the act of baptising. The river Jordan is symbolized by the austere old man sitting near a vase from which the river springs. This figure is characterized by two divine

Arian baptistery - Detail the Cupola (Vth cent.)

aquatic attributes: a green rush in his hand, and two red lobster claws above his head.

The encircling ring around this scene shows the twelve apostles two by two, led by St. Peter and St. Paul going towards a throne surmounted by a cross, this being the symbol of Christ's sovereignty). Each apostle, separated from the other by a palm-tree, carries jewelled crowns in his veiled hands, except St. Peter who carries the keys, and St. Paul a rolled manuscript. All this has a background of gold.

This mosaic shows two clear styles. The first, including the central medallion, the throne and St. Peter, St. Paul and the apostle behind the latter, shows a major vigour. The second includes the remaining nine apostles and though only a little later, it has more diffused and paler chromatic tones.

Baptistery of the Arians (6th cent.) - The Cupola

The Arian Baptistery

THE BASILICA OF ST. JOHN THE EVANGELIST

(Viale Farini)

This was built by the august Galla Placidia about 424 A.D., in the fulfillment of a vow after having escaped the dangers of a terrible tempest during the sea voyage from Constantinople together with her sons. The Basilica was seriously damaged by bombing during 1944, but was rebuilt immediately after the war, respecting the original structures of the apse and architecture of the facade, including the great medieval « Protiro » over the entrance door.

During the re-building, it was found that the church (49 m 72 cm. long and 22 m 20 cm. wide) was originally shorter, but a short time after its erection it included the narthex, and so became divided into three naves with two lines of twelve grey marble columns, not nine. The original pavement has been raised about 2 m 26 cm.

The Basilica is preceded by a quadrangle recently completely reconstructed, and now has a Gothic marble portal on the front, decorated with figures and a bas-relief.

The right hand nave contains the robust square bell-tower, 42 m 25 cm high, including the conical roof. Two of the bells were cast in 1208 by a certain Roberto Sassone.

S. Giovanni Evangelista - The Gothic portal

Church of St. Giovanni Evangelista

The inside of the Basilica is bathed in light coming from the numerous windows, and thus exalting the spatial values of the building giving a tone of calm spaciousness. The triumphal arch and apsidal dome are now covered with a white plaster, but from the V up to the XVI century they were adorned with splendid mosaics, ordered by Galla Placidia herself. One of the scenes on the archway showed the miraculous rescue of Galla Placidia's ship, by St. John the Evangelist, during the voyage from Constantinople after her brother Honorius had died.

The small loggetta with seven continuous openings in the apse is of great architectural interest. Its origins are controversial: but it seems that it is V century and not VIII or IX as some scholars say. Along the perimetral walls are various mosaic panels coming from the various strata of the pavement, which during the centuries has had to be raised to avoid the water coming from underneath. The mosaics on the left hand wall are of 1213 A.D. and narrate episodes from the IV crusade.

There are also popular scenes, such as the funeral of the foxes, and many other fantastic animals. The small chapel about halfway along the left nave is decorated with fourteenth century frescoes, probably carried out by Giovanni Baronzio. The frescoes show, the four Evangelists, and their symbols and the Elders of the church, St. Jerome, St. Ambrose, St. Augustine and St. Gregory.

S. APOLLINARE NUOVO

(Via di Roma)

Preceded by a Renaissance portico and flanked by a 38 m high cylindrical bell-tower with the famous mullioned windows increasing in aperture as they go higher, the Basilica which was built about 526 A.D. by king Theodoric, was destined to be used for the Arian cult and dedicated to the Redeemer. After the fall of the Goths, about 561, the church was changed to the Catholic cult and dedicated to St. Martin Archbishop of Tours.

During the IX century the church changed its name yet again, for the remains of S. Apollinare, which had been conserved in the Basilica outside Ravenna (Classe), were entrusted to it. Since then it has been called S. Apollinare Nuovo, meaning « New ». The inside of the 42 m 21 cm. long church is again divided into three naves by two lines of twelve marble columns each. These columns and the pavement were raised by 1.20 m above the original level in the XVI century. The apse, at the bottom of the centre nave was rebuilt in 1950 on the original walls brought to light during the restoration. Behind this there still remains the ample baroque apse. Along the dividing line between the centre nave and the apsidal space, there are three marble transennae and a pluteo.

The latter has a vase design with symmetric intertwin-

S. Apollinare Nuovo

S. Apollinare Nuovo - Interior

ing vines beside a cross, with a monogram, between two peacocks. The centre of the presbytery contains four porphyry columns with typical Byzantine capitals. Without doubt these formed part of the old **ciborium** covering the altar. The lacunar ceiling was built in the XVI century: the original was trussed allowing the golden lacunar along the slope of the roof to be seen, because the church was named, « In coelo aureo » (in the golden sky).

Originally the superb mosaic decorations also covered the apse and the opposite wall. Today, only the lateral ones along the central nave remain. These mosaics are in three horizontal strips or lines, above one another. The first, the highest near the ceiling, the second along the height of the windows and the lowest immediately above the arches supported by the columns.

All these mosaics are of the Theodoric period except the middle section of the lowest strip of each wall, which, according to the historian A. Agnello, are of the VI century when the church was reconciled to the Catholics. On the highest strip of the left hand wall, constantly alternating with panels containing shell shaped pavilions there follow thirteen panels showing the following scenes which, starting from the bottom, illustrate Christ's principal miracles and some parables: 1) the marriage feast (unfortunately this has been altered by a bad restoration carried out during the last century); 2) the multiplication of the bread and fish; 3) the calling of Peter and Andrew; 4) the healing of the blind; 5) the healing of the sick; 6) the Samaritan at the well; 7) the raising of Lazzarus; 8) the Pharasee and the Publican before the temple; 9) the widow's

mite; 10) Christ separating the sheep from the goats;
11) the healing of the paralytics of Copernaum; 12) the
healing of the possessed; 13) the healing of the paralytic
of Bethesda.

On the opposite side (right hand wall) the highest
strip, beginning at the end of the church, illustrates the
following scenes in thirteen panels, referring to the Passion
of Christ or the events immediately after His death: 1) the
last supper; 2) the prayer in the Garden of Gethseme; 3)
Judas' betrayal; 4) Christ taken prisoner; 5) Jesus before
the Sanhedrin; 6) the announcement of Peter's denial; 7)

S. Apollinare Nuovo - Marble « pluteo »

S. Apollinare Nuovo - The Virgins (6th cent.)

S. Apollinare Nuovo - Detail of the procession of martyrs (6th cent.)

S. Apollina
Nuovo -
«Transenn
large
carved
marble
panel

Peter's denial; 8) Judas' penitence; 9) Christ before Pilate in the act of washing his hands; 10) Christ taken to Calvary; 11) the good woman speaking to the angels; 12) the disciples on the way to Emmaus; 13) the appearance of Christ to the apostles and the doubts of Thomas.

The thirteen panels on the left are characterized by their stillness and formal balance. Those on the right, on the other hand, are a little more crowded with figures and present more drammatic scenes with greater movement. So it seems evident that the work was carried out by two different artistic temperaments.

S. Apollinare Nuovo - The call of Peter and Andrew (6th cent.)

The mosaics on the window-level (central strip) are given a golden background and show 32 figures of Saints and Prophets carrying rolled, or half open, or open manuscripts. The robustness with which these figures were modelled shows that the artist felt the fascination of form and volume.

The illustrations, at the beginning and end of the lowest strip, are of the Theodoric period too. These are: the Port and town of Classe and the Virgin Mary between four angels on the left, Theodoric's Palace and Christ between four angels on the right. The central figures of female Saints preceded by the three kings on the left, and martyrs on the right, are of the Justinian period.

The two long processions wind along at the same speed and with the same solemn pace recalling a slow psalm-like rhythm. This composition has the concept of a figurative Litany, as is made clear by the fact that each figure is identified by a name above it.

The so-called PALACE OF THEODORIC

(Via di Roma)

This very old building, commonly called Theodoric's Palace, is very near S. Apollinare. Some scholars have identified it with the «**Calchi**», an old name for a regiment of guards, others have identified it as a « **Sicreston** » or Exharcs' Office. Very probably it is the facade of the narthex of the medieval church dedicated to the Redeemer. Bounded on two sides by two pilaster strips, it has a slight central projection on the low parts with a great archway. The higher parts on the other hand, contain an ample niche curving round in the form of a balcony.

The sides of this facade are composed, low down, of two great twin mullioned windows, and higher up, by two blind porticoes, each supported by three small columns on a marble sill.

Theodoric's Palace

S. MARIA IN PORTO (in the town)

(Via di Roma)

This monumental Basilica, the inside of which measures 68 x 47,50 m, was built between 1553 and 1606. Much of the material comes from the very old church of the Honorian period, the church of « St. Lawrence in Cesarea ». The great facade of Istrian stone, adorned with semicolumns and statues, is in two parts, for the lowest of which, towards the end of the XVIII century, the architect C. Morigia, adopted a pre-existing plan.

The inside of the building, in Renaissance and Palladian style, is ample and solemn. It is divided into three naves by two lines of alternating columns and square pillars and is crowned by a hexagonal dome 48 m 16 cm. high. The high altar contains the famous bas-relief of the IX century showing the Virgin Mary, and is known as the « **Greek Madonna** ». According to the legend, it arrived on the sea-shore accompanied by two angels bearing flaming torches, at dawn, on the 8th of April 1100 A.D.

Behind the altar, running around the apse are the very fine wooden carved choir stalls, carried out between 1576 and 1593 by the Frenchman Maestro Marino.

The church of S. Maria in Porto

ACADEMY GALLERY

(in the Loggetta Lombardesca)

The opening of the picture gallery in Ravenna dates back to 1829. The collection of several works of art was carried out through the appeal which the vice-Legate Mons. Livinio de' Medici Spada, Ignazio Sarti, the Gonfalonier Conte Carlo Arrigoni addressed to all the inhabitants of Ravenna, and by the Cardinal Legate Agostino Rivarola's authoritative permission.

Most of Ravenna's nobles immediately answered that fair call. Planned by Ignazio Sarti and built in Via Bac-

Loggetta Lombardesca

carini, it became the seat for the fine arts Academy a few years later. Recently all the works of art and the Academy itself have been transferred to the « Loggia del Giardino », called « Loggetta Lombardesca ».

In this splendid monumental whole, enriched with a large brick building on each side, a superimposed order arcade formed by five quick and harmonious spans, stands out for its pretty shape.

It is the « Loggetta Lombardesca », so called for its having been worked on mainly by lombard marble-cutters of the early sixteenth century.

Placed behind it is the large, double-arched cloister of the former S. Maria in Porto Monastery, built in the early sixteenth century.

Guidarello Guidarelli (detail)

Galleria dell'Accademia · Antonio Vivarini · The Crucifixion

The number of paintings displayed in the Academy Gallery dates back from thirteenth to twentieth century.

Also to be particularly noted are the paintings by artists from the Romagnola school, such as Nicolò Rondinelli, a Renaissance painter follower of Giovanni Bellini and author of a beautiful altar-piece representing the Virgin Mary between S. Caterina and S. Girolamo, crowned by two angels; Francesco Zaganelli from Cotignola, an early seventeenth century artist, with his original « Shepherds' Worship »; Luca Longhi who portrayed Captain Raffaele Rasponi and doctor Giovanni Arrigoni in the second half of XVI century.

Among the valuable pictures from other schools you can find Guercino's « S. Romualdo », Palmezzano's Nativity, Presentation to the temple, Ludovico Carracci's Christ's head, Antonio Vivarini's Crucifixion.

The marble statue of the soldier Guidarello Guidarelli, dead in 1501 at Imola, is placed within a large hall with fine paintings.

The work was done by Tullio Lombardi in 1525 and first of all is noteworthy for its features' delicacy contrasting with the stiffness of the armour enclosing the whole body.

As D'Annunzio wrote in his Laudi, the young knight was represented:

**...asleep lying on his back with folded arms
on his wide sword.
His motionless face bore the seal of iron,
death and suffering...**

S. Apollinare in Classe
Excavations of the Basilica 1½ miles south
off S. Apollinare in Classe
Excavation of the church of S. Severo
Theodoric's mausoleum

*

SANT'APOLLINARE IN CLASSE

Bishop Maximian, whose fortunate lot it had been to consecrate S. Vitale, shortly afterwards—on May 9th, 549—also consecrated the large imposing basilica of S. Apollinare in Classe. The name « in Classe » derives from the neighbouring « oppidum Classis », the town which sprang up in defence of the famous Port founded by Augustus. And it was to the inhabitants of this « castrum » or fort, who were mainly merchants and seamen, that S. Apollinaris, the first Bishop of Ravenna, brought the good tidings of the new Faith, the comforting words of the Gospel. We do not know exactly when he lived: it is hardly likely that we must go back so far as the age of the Apostles, as is suggested in the « Passio S. Apollinaris », a legendary narrative drawn up probably at the end of the 5th or at the beginning of the 6th century (Mazzotti). The desire to go back to this ancient time

S. Apollinare in Classe

S. Apollinare in Classe · Interior

shows that the hagiographer, while wishing to ennoble the figure of the first Bishop, tried at the same time to shed further glory upon the origin of the church of his city.

Very soon cemeteries arose around the town of Classe, and these were in part used by the Christians, as can be proved from the discovery there of various funerary inscriptions. Beside, rather than upon, one of these burying grounds, as De Rossi has thought, Bishop Ursicinus, in the second quarter of the 6th century, built the magnificent church of Classe which now stands almost alone (at least for the present) in the midst of the country, whilst behind it, towards the sea, stretches the dark green of that vast pine wood « spessa e viva » (thick and living) of which Dante and Byron sang.

The Church is about four miles from the centre of Ravenna, and is now far from the sea which was at one time very near it. It can be seen from afar, not so much by reason of its imposing mass, as for the tall and massive Campanile (123 ft. high), belonging perhaps to the end of the 10th century, which is rendered more slender and graceful in appearance by the ascending series of windows—the lowest with a single opening (« monofore »), the next above with two openings (« bifore »), and the third with three («trifore»). In these latter there are white columns with characteristic crutch-shaped capitals.

Julianus Argentarius, who financed the construction of S. Vitale, undertook the considerable task of building this church too, and it is for that reason that one sees here the long thin red bricks which are to be seen in all Julianus's other edifices.

This church, which has the usual basilican form, at first had an atrium in front of it, as is proved by the fact that some remains of it were discovered last century. To the central block of the façade, flanked on their side by two smooth uprights, is added the narthex which has on its left a high quadrangular building which has been a great deal restored. There must also have been a similar structure on the right, for it has been possible to trace its foundations.

A rhythmical design of blind arches supported by uprights enlivens the side walls of the exterior, in which there are numerous wide windows. The apse, semicircular inside, is polygonal outside. Beside the apse stand the two square chapels known as the « prothesis » and the « diaconicon », each of which has a small pentagonal apse.

The interior (182 ft. by 99 ft.) is spacious and solemn, and is impressive especially for the great width of the central nave, which is flanked by two rows of magnificent marble columns from the workshops of Proconnesos. They are marked by horizontal veining, are raised upon square bases and are surmounted by capitals carved with leaves that seem blown out by the wind. Above the capitals are « pulvini ». The whole of this material shows the most homogeneous uniformity of style and measurement, so that there is no doubt that it was expressly ordered for the erection of this church.

The side walls, in each of which there were originally three doors, are now a bare and unadorned expanse of brick, but once they were covered with panels of polished marble, for Andrea-Agnello writes in his « Liber Pontifi-

† OTHO III ROM. IMP. GERM. OB PATRATA CRIMINA AVSTERIORI
DISCIPLINAE SANCTI ROMVALDI OBTEMPERANS EMENSO NVDIS PEDI
BVS AB VRBE ROMA AD GARGANVM MONTEM ITINERE BASILICAM
HANC ET COENOBIVM CLASSENSE XXXX DIEBVS POENITENS INHABITA
VIT ET HIC CILICIO AC VOLVNTARIIS CASTIGATIONIBVS PECCATA SVA
EXPIANS AVGVSTVM DEDIT HVMILITATIS EXEMPLVM ET IMPERATOR
SIBI TEMPLVM HOC ET POENITENTIAM SVAM NOBILITAVIT ANO P.C.M.

S. Apollinare in Classe - Sarcophagus of the Archbishop Teodoro

S. Apollinare in Classe - The Apse (6th cent.)

S. Apollinare in Classe - St. Apollinaris (6th cent.)

calis Ecclesiae Ravennatis », that no church in Italy was so rich in valuable stones—« in lapidibus preciosis »—. These marbles were in great part carried away in the first half of the 15th century when Sigismondo Pandolfo Malatesta asked for and obtained them to decorate the church at Rimini which took its name from him.

The choir of the church is now raised well above the level of the nave: this is due to the addition below it of the crypt, which is semicircular in form with a central corridor. Some critics think it was built in the 7th century (Grabar), according to others (Mazzotti) towards the end of the 9th, while yet others (Ricci) attribute it to the second half of the 12th. In any case it is certain that when the basilica was built, instead of the raised choir, there was the « bema », or enclosure reserved for the clergy; this extended towards the centre of the edifice as far as the two third columns from the further end. In fact, its foundations—upon which must have rested the carved sections and small marble pilasters for the parapet surrounding it—were brought to light in 1953 about one foot below the level of the present flooring, as the result of certain careful investigations.

Of the ancient mosaic pavement which must have co-vered the whole of this vast building like an immense carpet, a few remains have been found at the end of the left aisle, and at the beginning of the right. Here an expanse of mosaic, showing geometrical designs, preserves an inscription recording that a great part of this work was done at her personal expense by a certain lady « Gauden-tia », and a certain « Felix », together with other bene-

S. Apollinare in Classe - Face of Christ at center of the Cross

factors. Another fragment of mosaic, discovered in 1953 below the flooring of the central nave, has been affixed to the right wall of the church.

But the thing which most arrests the attention of the visitor as he enters the church of S. Apollinare in Classe, is without doubt the sumptuous many-coloured mantle of mosaic which covers the choir arch and the semidome of the apse.

Not all this mosaic, however, belongs to the same period. The upper part of the arch would seem to go back, according to some scholars (Toesca) to the 7th century, but according to others (Galassi) it is to be attributed to the 9th. In the upper part, which stretches horizontally over the whole width above the arch, is a figure of Christ with wide open eyes and wrinkled brow, within a medallion. Beside him, in the midst of a sea of stylised clouds, are the winged symbols of the Evangelists, the Eagle, the Man, the Lion and the Bull; in the last figure it is to be noticed that the head is drawn strictly in profile but the nostrils appear to be in a perfectly frontal position. The zone below these figures shows on the extreme right and left the two symbolical cities of Jerusalem and Bethlehem, their walls adorned with precious stones. From their gates issue twelve lambs, six on each side, which advance upwards towards the Christ in the medallion above; we have here undoubtedly a symbolic representation of the twelve Apostles.

In the narrow spaces beside the arch two palm trees stand out on a dark blue background. This part of the mosaic is to be assigned to the 6th century, as are also

S. Apollinare in Classe · Apse (detail)

the figures below representing the **Archangels Gabriel and Michael,** who, like celestial warriors, carry the « labarum » or banner bearing the praise of the Thrice Holy God. Lower still we see the figures belonging to the 12th century (Toesca) of St. Matthew and, perhaps, St. Luke.

The entire decoration of the dome of the apse is to be attributed to about the middle of the 6th century. The composition, based on the agreement of colours few but bright, falls naturally into two parts. Above, upon a sky of gold streaked by many small clouds, stands a great jewelled disc which contains a cross studded with many precious stones; this, in its turn, at the point where the arms cross, bears within a circle the head of Christ. The upper part of the cross is surmounted by the Greek word IXΘYC; the word means «fish» and the letters of the Greek word stand for the initial letters of « Jesus Christ Son of God Saviour ». Beneath the cross we read the words: « Salus Mundi » i.e. Salvation of the World.

This great medallion is flanked by the figures of Moses and Elijah emerging from the clouds. Their presence clearly proves that the artist is alluding to the Transfiguration of Christ on Mt. Tabor, which was witnessed by the Apostles Peter, James and John, whom we must recognize as being represented symbolically by the three white lambs which stand below but raise their heads towards the jewelled cross.

Lower down the zone widens out into a green flowery valley, varied by the emergence of small dark rocks bordered with white, and enlivened by a luxuriant growth of

146

S. Apollinare in Classe - Sarcophagus of the « Twelve Apostles »

grass, bushes and other plants among which we may see the pine—the tree which is still today especially characteristic of the countryside around Ravenna. In the centre of this scene, which has a soft shade of green for background, stands the tall, solemn imposing figure of St. Apollinaris wearing, over his white alb, the chasuble adorned with many golden bees—the symbol of eloquence. The first Bishop of Ravenna is in the attitude of an « orans » i.e. he is pictured at the moment of uttering his prayers that God will grant his heavenly grace to the faithful entrusted to his care who are here seen as twelve lambs that surround him. It is for this reason that the composition might almost be said to be inspired by the last words of the sermon which St. Peter Chrysologus preached in honour of St. Apollinaris: « Ecce vivit, ecce ut bonus Pastor suo medio assistit in grege » (Behold he lives, behold how the good Shepherd stands in the midst of his flock).

The figures of the Bishops Severus, Ecclesius, Ursus and Ursicinus clad in their sacred vestments, which are seen in the spaces between the windows, are contemporary with the building of the church.

The two panels seen at the side of the apse are a little more than a century later: in the right we see the Sacrifices of Abel, Abraham and Melchizedek where the composition is not devoid of balance, but the colours are weak and undecided. On the left are the Emperor Constantine IV Pogonatus (the bearded) with his brothers Heraclius and Tiberius in the act of handing the rescript of « Privileges » to Reparatus, the delegate of Archbishop

S. Apollinare in Classe - Sarcophagus of the Apostles: the right side

S. Apollinare in Classe - The marble canopy

Maurus. The work reechoes the one seen on the panels of the apse of S. Vitale, but during the course of centuries, it has undergone various alterations, so that today we see it almost all restored in tempera to imitate mosaic.

These are some important sarcophagi lining the side walls of the church. They belong to the 5th, 6th, 7th and 8th centuries, and by taking them in turn one can gain an idea of the development of sculpture throughout this period. One notices how, from the sculptured figures of the Apostles which in the art of Ravenna are typical of the 5th century one passes in the next century and those that follow, to representations in which their symbolical and decorative character is increased by the lack of modelling, and indeed by a very marked flatness.

Also worthy of note is the marble canopy over the altar at the further end of the left aisle; from the inscription around the upper border we learn that it was erected at the beginning of the 9th century in honour of the third Bishop of Ravenna St. Eleucadius. Beneath the canopy, and affixed to the wall, are two small marble panels showing the Annunciation; in one the Angel advances with his staff and stretching out his hand as he speaks; in the other the Virgin is seen seated in the act of spinning purple thread. These two small panels are to be assigned, not so much to the 7th century as some have said (Gerspach), as to the 10th.

S. Apollinare in Classe - Sarcophagus of the lambs

EXCAVATIONS OF THE BASILICA
1½ MILES FROM S. APOLLINARE IN CLASSE

(Near the locality called « Ca' Bianca », it is about 800 m west of State highway N° 16)

Near Classe (south-south east of Ravenna) during the Paleochristian period numerous churches were built. The only remaining one that is structurally complete is S. Apollinare in Classe. In 1965, Cortesi found the remains of a church in the locality called « **Cà Bianca** », and as it is about eight km. from Ravenna it is thought to be that of S. Demetrio. (The historian Agnello tells us that it was six miles from Ravenna).

The excavations, (still unfinished) have brought to light the foundation of a 44 m x 31 x 50 m basilica, preceded by a 20 m long entrance hall. The church had three naves, and it seems it was flanked by two long rectangular buildings, probably functioning as ambulatories or porticoes. Perhaps these were added later.

The proportions of this church are very similar to those of S. Apollinare Nuovo, so it may follow that the building was Arian, thus being of the V or VI century. Numerous fragments of pavement mosaic found here have been transferred on to slabs of cement and may now be seen in the National Museum in Ravenna.

A few yards from the northern flank of the basilica, are the remains of an octagonal building, (internal width of 9 m) which could be identified as a baptistry not a mausoleum. The true function of this building will only be made certain after systematic archeological exploration.

S. SEVERO

(Reached by the Adriatic State highway N° 16 halfway between Ponte Nuovo on the Fiumi Uniti, and S. Apollinare in Classe.)

The foundations of this church — the plan of which was brought to light by the scholar Cortesi by hand-drilling during the winter of 1963-64 — was systematically uncovered during the summer excavations between 1964 and 1967 by Bermond-Montanari of the « Soprintendenza alle Antichità dell'Emilia Romagna ».

These excavations are half way between S. Apollinare in Classe and the Fiumi Uniti and between the Rimini-Ravenna railway line and the Adriatic State highway N° 16. The exact site of this church is now easily found, because there are the remains of an early medieval square bell-tower, also visible from the highway.

This church, begun under the episcopacy of Peter II (570-577 A.D.) was finished under his successor bishop John III (578-594 A.D.). The latter transferred here the remains of St. Severo, twelfth bishop of Ravenna, who until then had lain in the oratory of St. Rufillo, brought to light in October 1967, by the southern flank of the church. Preceded by a rectangular narthex, the Basilica (50 m x 30) seems to have been divided into three naves and had a mosaic pavement with a geometric design.

These mosaics, preserved on slabs of cement, are now to be seen in the National Museum. Under the old pavement of the church, are the remains of a mosaic floor belonging to a Roman villa.

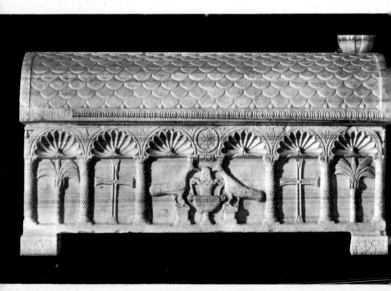

S. Apollinare in Classe · Sarcophagus with six niches

THEODORIC'S MAUSOLEUM

(Via delle Industrie)

About ½ mile north-east of Ravenna is the austere and imposing Mausoleum of Theodoric king of the Goths, who died in 526. He wanted to build the Mausoleum himself, and, according to a contemporary writer, looked for an enormous stone (**ingens saxum**) for the roof.

The roof is in fact made of one single piece measuring 11 m diameter and about 3 m thick, so its weight is about 300 tons. The whole construction is of well-cut grey Istrian granite and blocks without mortar, using the dry-wall system. The building is divided into two levels, one above the other.

The lower, decagonal in shape, has an ample niche on each side. Over these there are archways formed by hewn stone. The western niche contains the door leading to a cross shaped room lit by six tiny windows; by observing these windows one can see the considerable thickness of the walls.

This room was probably a chapel for the funeral rites. The second level is a little smaller and this too, is decagonal becoming circular towards the roof. Under the single piece of the roof runs a typical nordic motif called «**tenaille**». The roof, used to seal the royal Mausoleum, has twelve

157

Theodoric's Grave (6th cent.)

Theodoric's portrait
on the gold medallion
coming from
Senigallia,
now in the National
Roman Museum

stone handles at equal distances, which were probably used as anchors for the ropes when it was put into position.

According to a recent technical study, the roof was raised to the height of the second level by the use of a ramp, and then lifted by levers. The inside of the second level is completely circular and contains a red porphyry bath used as Theodoric's coffin.

Returning to the roof one can see that it is cracked into two separate parts. According to legend, this was caused by lightning. Theodoric had been informed by an oracle that he would be struck by lightning, and during a terrible storm when he was taking shelter in the Mausoleum, lightning struck, passed through the roof and killed him.

INDEX

tipo-lito stimmatini - verona